A DREAM OF DONKEYS

by

Jenny Sparks

ISBN 978 0 86071 662 4

British Library Cataloguing in Publication Data.
A catalogue record for this book is available
from the British Library.

A Commissioned Publication

tel: 0115 932 0643 web: www.moorleys.co.uk

To Cass and Peter, who have given
this dream a perfect ending.

*Collective terms are the stuff of Trivia quizzes; for example, the very
descriptive 'An Exaltation of Larks' or better still 'A Crash of Rhinos'.
You would stump up everyone with 'A Dream of Donkeys' but
necessity is the mother of invention and I needed a title.*

CHAPTER 1
GENESIS

I hadn't spilt a drop of iodine as I went over backwards, felled by Sophie's flashing hooves as she fired both barrels. She had caught me fair and square in the stomach and I landed on the flinty floor of the old sheep house where she'd elected to foal. By a miracle I hadn't hit my head, but I wasn't out of trouble yet. Her wild-eyed glare warned me to keep my distance, and not try any more funny business.

Somehow I got up out of the way and retired from the fray, hurt and thoroughly put in my place. As far as I was concerned her baby's navel would have to dry up on its own. Fortunately it looked O.K. and mother and child were well. So I made a quick exit. Passing the rest of the donkeys who had witnessed this drama, I realised they were very wisely keeping their distance. In fact, for several days we all gave Sophie and the infant a wide berth.

Her over-protective mothering was impressive, but could well have been triggered by events which occurred while she was in Ireland. I was to learn that, had she produced a colt foal the previous year, it would have been immediately taken away from her and disposed of. Rearing it would have been too expensive, as feed costs had rocketed and only females were being kept. By the time Sophie and her friends came to me, she was herself destined for slaughter as the situation had worsened.

Once back at the house, still clutching my pot of iodine, I took stock. The biggest injury was to my pride and I had to smile as memories of 70 years ago began to flood into my mind. My father was laughing (and how he would just have done) and I at all of three years, was stamping my foot and saying, "I will! **I will!!**" My 'Impossible Dream' had just had a painful birth and no wonder! For we lived in a Grocer's shop on the A5, with traffic thundering past, day and night. All we had was a backyard, with a few hollyhocks. We were complete 'Townies' and to cap it all, my mother was a model and buyer for Harrods, no child of hers could go down the route I had in mind.

But our very situation constantly re-inforced my determination to "Move to the country near the sea and have a farm!", as I had told my Dad that day. I was to see beloved cats and dogs killed on the road and I hated it. Worse still two sisters, clients of the shop, who I adored as 'Aunties', were killed one night, by the same Lorry.

I loved the seaside, where, as a family we would go on a Sunday, quite regularly, despite the 90-mile journey, in our ancient Ford Popular. (Black of course!) I'd only seen a farm in books, but I'd begun to collect a model one and each day I sorted out the 'stock' into the fields. I had cattle, working horses, sheep, poultry, cats and dogs and of course, donkeys. I was caring for them and keeping them safe. Although I could not have expressed the idea then, in my mind it was to be a Sanctuary for tame and wild life. Even mice of which I'm very fond, featured in this plan, but I certainly didn't mention them to my father! Mice and Grocer's shops simply don't go together.

Well, ... I never voiced my dream again for many years, but it would not go away. Our Father God had singled me out to be a Cowsbody, indeed a Sheepsbody and Donkeysbody. He had seen to it that it was written in my D.N.A. I couldn't escape my destiny, chosen in His plans before I even came to be.[1] He saw to it that certain events would strengthen my resolve. The first was a visit to my best friend's grandparents. They had a smallholding in a tiny village called Potten End. There was probably only an acre or so of land, but to me, at five, it was enormous and above all there was a pony, poultry and peace. On arriving home I told my father "I've been to Heaven to-day" at which he laughed again. He was a terrible tease but at five my sense of humour didn't extend to my precious dream.

The second life-changing milestone was my Mother's death at 41 of tuberculosis. Somehow I had got to deal this dying business, for four and two-leggeds alike.

My father had no suggestions, but to get some peace and quiet he packed me off to the weekly Youth Fellowship at our local church. All part of God's plan of course, because there I found the answer! The leader, who loved the Lord Jesus as his friend and saviour, showed me how Jesus had rescued all of us, all His created life, from death and decay,[2] by dying and then conquering death by His resurrection in which we can all share. By trusting in Him, we will live forever in a restored paradise. So now as then, when I bury a beloved four-legged or a dear, two-legged friend I can say, "Goodbye for now, I'll see you in Heaven." And I know it will be a lot better than Potten End!

[1.] Psalm 139:16.   [2.] Romans 8:20,21 TLB (The Living Bible)

2

CHAPTER 2
A PRIDE OF OWLS

"There are four owlets in here Jenny! Not just two as you thought," John told me triumphantly. Putting each one in a tiny sack, he climbed down from the Owl Box which is high up on a main beam in the Big Barn. Then he carefully extricated them, one by one and ringed them giving me a chance to stroke those soft feathers and exult in their beauty.

"You've certainly won the prize for Barn Owl care this year, it was worth all your effort Jenny," John told me, as he recounted the struggles the birds had faced. What with the coldest winter for I don't know how many years, and then the driest spring in living memory, many Barn Owls hadn't made it. Others hadn't laid and the largest hatching he had seen was two. So, that 20 foot climb each day, to feed the chicks and adults had paid off. It does not come easy to me, because I inherited my father's fear of heights. Even standing on a chair can freak me out, so I never added a ladder to that Model Farm. And I have to confess that I felt rather proud of myself and you know what happens then ....

That takes me back a while to when Andrew, a farming friend and I were sailing one morning on our local estuary. It was a breezy day, so we decided to take the 'Dolly's' boat and sail together. Between us, we were quite confident that we could manage the tricky wind and keep upright – no problem! I had dressed rather casually; both of us had our buoyancy aids on, but I'd just worn jeans and a baggy sweater.

As we reached the sea entrance we had to make a tack (i.e. change direction). As I pushed the tiller over, you can perhaps guess what happened next. The thin extension handle, which you see use when having to sit out on the gunwale in strong winds, shot straight up my sleeve. We then gyrated at high speed, gibing over and over again, with the boom clouting Andrew's head. Disgusted at being sailed so incompetently, the dinghy managed to jerk the tiller out and throw me over the stern. The last Andrew saw of me was a pair of feet going vertically down. Pride had certainly come before a fall![1] As I gurgled to the surface the full horror of our situation hit me. It was an ebbing tide and I would soon be swept off to Germany. Andrew and the boat had gone off in the opposite direction with him nursing a sore head and with little idea of how to sail alone. On top of all that there was no one else on the estuary to come to our aid or dial up the Coastguard. I'm no great swimmer either and after a few strokes I realised I'd never reach the shore.

At that point my feet touched the bottom! I was on a sandbank and to my relief and amazement Andrew had turned the boat round, leapt off and turned it into the wind, so we could climb back on board. We crept home with me feeling thoroughly ashamed of myself at putting us both in such danger. As I reviewed things later and thanked God for His grace and our safety, David's words in Psalm 40 became mine. "He lifted me ... and set my feet on a rock and gave me a firm place to stand, he put a new song in my mouth, a hymn of praise."

What has all this to do with the Barn Owls? Well, having boasted to a few people about 'my' four owlets and how they'd grown (two large females and two smaller males) I should have known better. A month after John's joyful discovery, I went out to the cattle to check their water tank, and there, to my horror, was a Barn Owl, he'd drowned overnight, a male fledgling. So beautiful, so rare and so very dead. How I mourned for him and felt so responsible.

Of course I was responsible, over the tank. I have tried providing a lifeline for any luckless bird or mammal that has tumbled into the water, but the bulls always manage to dislodge the sack or whatever.

But my responsibility for the owl's death goes beyond this. I along with all mankind, in our natural rebellion against accountability to our Creator, brought death into the world – see the early chapters of Genesis. Our desire to know evil, as well as good, could not go on. No right-minded person wants an Eternal Holocaust, or war or endless cruelty, abuse and exploitation. But our Creator Lord "died to reconcile all things to Himself"[2]. The Greek means all life; so He will restore Owl and I shall see him flying free again.

[1] Proverbs 16:18. [2] Colossians 1:20

4

CHAPTER 3
TWO THIRDS FULL

At three years old I didn't know anything about sailing (or Barn Owls for that matter) and although I love the sea, swimming is not my strong point. I have never been able to master the crawl; in fact I go best on my back. As it happened, this was also true of Michael, my husband. In public pools we had to clear a path for each other to avoid drowning anyone and it caused much confusion!

Despite this ineptness, we loved being on the water. Mike had learned to sail in his early teens, on the Norfolk Broads. This was in the days of no buoyancy aids for either people or boats – Health and Safety would have a fit now! He was to teach me how to handle a boat once we moved to North Norfolk very soon after marrying. We had achieved $^2/_3$ of my Dream; we were "in the country and near the sea", because Michael shared this longing too. We had bought a property with an acre or so, because he wanted to create his Dream, of a landscaped garden, self-sufficient in fruit and vegetables and with a small plant nursery. He was a member of the Royal Horticultural Society and grew many rare trees, shrubs and plants. But of course this couldn't earn us a living and so we both took up teaching posts at a nearby Grammar School. We had fled the A5 and the town we were born in to settle in a rural idyll.

For 18 years we lived by the source of the River Burn and knew the joys of hearing lapwings calling, snipe drumming, larks exalting and water rails chirruping. We could watch kingfishers fishing and water voles just messing about in the river.

Soon after we moved from there the whole area dried up and the wild life we were so privileged to enjoy has disappeared. Why? Because irrigation on a huge scale for the intensive farming around has sucked the area dry.

This was definitely not the kind of agriculture I had in mind at all. In my eyes no farm is complete without cattle and although I had not yet met a cow or bull face to face, I knew they were the key to unlocking that elusive $^1/_3$ of The Dream.

So that's how we came to be proud owners of a goat! Wrong key I know, but the nearest I could find to try; so Sarah came to us as an animate lawnmower, because Michael's garden had a design fault. There was a surplus of rough grass and guess who'd had to mow it? She was a black and

5

white Alpine who would definitely have been happier in Switzerland! Despite my love and attention, she was lonely for her own kind and on top of that we were away from home through the weekdays. She would somehow pull up her tether and after ravaging our rose beds or flower borders she'd pay our neighbours a visit. This did not go down well and both our gardens were beginning to show the strain.

The day when we parted with her was mixed with sadness and relief, and in stark contrast to her arrival. We had driven her home in the back of our Morris Traveller – you know the sort – wooden framed and roomy. We had come home through Walsingham the very day of the annual mass pilgrimage. The march was completely disrupted as everyone spotted Sarah staring out the windows. We all laughed, but this made her nervous and the inevitable happened. Not surprisingly, no one was keen to have a lift with us in that particular vehicle afterwards.

So I was back in the role of mower-in-chief, in fact I'd never lost the job, as goats are not great fans of grass! The Impossible Dream was as far away as ever, but I'd not let it go. If you have such a one unfulfilled too, don't give up – not if God's put it there. Look at these words He gave to Habakkuk, for the Jews and you and me, "The vision awaits an appointed time ... though it lingers wait for it, it will certainly come."[1] That's a Promise!

[1] Habakkuk 2:3

6

CHAPTER 4
REBIRTH

Have you ever tried barrowing a hundredweight of milk in two tall containers down a steep track covered in ice over rutted snow? It's an exciting challenge and I've named it the "Dairy Cresta Run" and wonder if it could become a new Winter Olympic Sport. I wouldn't recommend you trying it, unless you have to. During the last two winters I had no choice. I was rearing bull calves, fifty or so, with some of them still on milk for a couple of months.

Now I'm the sort who can fall over a matchstick, so this kind of sledging was not up my street. It wouldn't have been so bad if the milk stayed still, but as it slops about, the journey becomes even more hazardous. And should the whole lot go over sideways and the lids fly off you literally <u>do</u> cry over spilt milk. Actually, you can be reduced to saying things best not repeated.

At least while there is snow about, the dangers are obvious, but if black ice forms it's a different story. And that takes me back to a life-changing February morning and yes, I was in my 40th year! The Dream was about to have a rebirth and it was going to be painful again!

At that time I was teaching 30 miles from home and late as usual, I and my little dog were dashing off, out the front door down the two steps. Rather quicker this morning as ice had formed over-night and our feet slipped from under us. The back of my head smashed down on to the second step and the bang was so horrendous, it haunted me for days. As I passed out, I could see my arms and legs flopping down though I felt nothing more. Michael, who left for school much later, was in mid-munch on his toast – hearing the racket he rushed out exactly like us, but had a softer landing on top of me.

After a trip to A & E and stitches put in my broken head, the full impact of the damage hit me. My balance was badly affected and some 'friends' unkindly said my brain too! Especially as the events which followed seemed to reinforce their conclusion. As I couldn't teach for a while and was confined to barracks, I idly switched on the T.V. one lunchtime and POW! The Dream's Green Light had come on! A woman's herd of Rare Breed Dexter Cows were featured – cows which are the smallest in the Western World. At 6 to 7 cwt they are half the size of a Simmental or Holstein and can almost stand under their bellies. "Yes! Yes!" I shouted to the T.V. We could fit one in Michael's landscaped garden, as easy as a goat. Known as the 'Smallholders Cow' they are very thrifty and produce rich milk and butter and are very efficient lawn mowers.

Perhaps you can picture Mike's face when I announced my news. But he thought: 'Poor soul, she's not well, she'll forget about it soon. In the meantime I'll humour her.'

Six months later we were on our way home with my cow, which we'd found in Surrey. And the journey was turning into a nightmare, because the huge trailer (plus the 7cwt giant cavorting about inside) was proving too much for our old car. (Just imagine towing a caravan with an Ogre lumbering about in it.) Its gears began giving out and we crawled home, with the clutch slipping and burning.

I also had other worries on my mind – the chief one being how to handle Woodmagic Moorhen out of the trailer and get her safely in our garden. She knew nothing of halters or commands, and she would be scared and bewildered. But once we had made it home she, like me, was so shocked and stunned, that she crept along after me, till we were safe at last.

Woodmagic Moorhen who started it all

8

I did get a rope on her, by the way. I dived over the back of the trailer, so we didn't have to open it before she was securely on a halter. Unfortunately I was wearing open-toed sandals; I didn't ever make that mistake again!

She had never been hand-milked and I'd only 'learned' the night before, practising on a friend's long-suffering Jersey Cow. She'd left her daughter of five months and all her sisters, cousins and aunts behind, so she was lonely. I became her 'herd' and in a week, she had learnt her name, accepted haltering, leading, even along our lane's verges, and my fumblings at milking. I had discovered that the way to her heart was through her stomach and since she had four of them we got through a lot of goodies.

At 6½ years she was in-calf again to a Pedigree Dexter and 6 months after coming to us, she had a copy book calving and gave me my first baby heifer. How I loved her! Little Amber, black like her Mum, was soon on a halter and walking along with me like a dog. A year later Moorhen was to produce another little girl after a very bad time for mother and baby (valuable experience for me). Beryl joined her sister to form our Pedigree herd – named after precious stones and minerals as I am a geographer and geologist. The Dexter tagging system had got to the A year, when Amber was born, so each succeeding year I used their letter for names. Hence B = Beryl (and C = Coral, Crystal etc.) But I'm jumping ahead!

So there we were with one cow, a rather naughty teenage heifer and another baby. Michael's garden was battle scarred and causing him much despair as MY cows caused more and more chaos. (Moorhen had been OUR cow, while Mike first began enjoying her delicious milk, butter and cheese, but the novelty had worn off). For his sanity we had to find more land. So the search was on and the Dream was burgeoning like an acorn..... God was way ahead of us and we had to get a move on to keep up. That dramatic February morning had shown us that Romans chapter 8 v28 is still in His Book.

"We know that all that happens to us is working for our good, if we love God and are fitting into His plans." *T.L.B.*

CHAPTER 5

CROSSROADS

The two gates either side of the lane were open and I was ready to lead the 50 strong flock of pregnant ewes out to their breakfast, across the road. Going to the door of the sheephouse I called them to me, using individual names and their group call of "Woollies". Knowing my voice and daily ready to follow me, they gathered round. By the way, if I'd sent you to collect them, they would have fled to the very back of the 100-foot barn at the first sight of a stranger. Nothing personal of course, just the wisdom and wariness of sheep, who only trust their shepherd. Surely a lesson for us here, who follow 'THE SHEPHERD'.

Having listened carefully for any traffic, and satisfied we were safe to go, I opened up and strode confidently ahead, shaking the food sack to encourage everyone to keep with me. Once in the field, I began spreading their roots out but... wait a minute.... several ewes were missing! Rushing back to the road I could see that about 20 of them had made a dreadful mistake. They were a ¼ of a mile away hurtling off in the direction of the village. Soon they'd reach a blind bend and on such a narrow, single track lane disaster could be imminent. There was no hope of catching up with the runaways and in any case, they in terror would have gone even faster. The only solution was to bellow at the top of my voice and rattle the sack. Some stopped looked back and saw me and a dear old faithful ewe, Mitey Min who'd joined me. Thankful that they could see their shepherd, they began running back, with all the rest joining in. Their closeness to me had saved the day and averted a catastrophe. They had no idea of what might have been ahead and I'll add nor do we, even from day to day. We're as vulnerable as any sheep.[1]

Michael and I certainly began walking in a property minefield as we searched for somewhere else to live, to suit us and our little Dexter herd, still growing, as Moorhen and now Amber too, were both in-calf. There were pitfalls a plenty ahead, but at least we had priorities; sufficient land and the right location of course.

One place which was tempting in its value in acreage but was 25 miles inland, is a good example of the snags we faced. I decided to view it on my own, while Mike was at school. I was to discover that it had a 1½-mile 'driveway', shared with a neighbouring farm. I and Sam my dog had crept along, trying but failing, to avoid the enormous potholes on the track. My car had not enjoyed the trip and I was still shaking when I climbed out. I must have looked rather shell-shocked, because I was greeted by the Vendor with, "You don't need to worry about the track!" But WE DID! If we had ever taken our beautiful wooden racing dinghy along it, just once, it would have become matchsticks! And we would have run up some impressive bills on broken car suspensions too!

Then we saw it! A tiny advert in the local paper for a farmhouse and 1 acre of land. The photo was minuscule and unimpressive, but despite the small acreage we knew it was right. On viewing it we persuaded the farmer to include the 6-acre field surrounding the house. He had just bought the 120 acres that made up Station Farm, and also swallowed up another farm the other side of the village. This was so he was now the proud owner of 1,000 acres (the goal at that time for any farmer of note). The house was surplus to his plans and its sale was to pay for some of the land he'd purchased.

It stood all alone in a pasture, just as our previous property had done. The site was ripe for landscaping, but this time Michael was only allowed half an acre, and even that he often had to share with a sheep or two. The location was perfect – 5 miles from where we lived before and much nearer the sea. It is a mile out of the village, beside what was once a railway line and train station, now a home. When the wind is in the north you can hear the tide breaking over the sand banks of Scolt Head Island. The farm nestles in a dry valley on a tiny lane, as far away from the A5 as you could imagine. It was another Taste of Heaven, but God's plans (and my dreams) were not complete by any means. The acorn had sprouted and the tree was growing.

---

[1] James 4:14

12

CHAPTER 6
THE OSTRIA

We'd just slept through poor Michael Fish's hurricane of 1987, blissfully unaware of the devastation that had been going on in Southern England that night. But as we came to, and heard the raging of the terrific gale, I remembered my Ostria! Leaping out of bed and rushing to the window, I could see it was horizontal and in danger of snapping. As Mike joined me he began to shout very severely and unkindly to it.... "You've had it! I'm never staking you anymore" and more words to that effect!

You see, ever since it had arrived from Hilliers Nurseries, the only place we had been able to track such a tree down, it had been a problem. Being very tall and with hardly any rootstock, it was a poor specimen, nothing like the magnificent tree I had seen in the photo I'd found in one of Mike's books. An Ostria is a hop hornbeam and has an elegant branching habit somewhat elm-like and covered with seeds like Chinese lanterns which turn golden in the autumn... And I <u>had</u> to have one.

As soon as I could I was outside pathetically trying to pull it up and tie it back. This brought Mike out to help; taking back his earlier outburst and fetching two iron stakes he supported it as never before. It was make or break time and the tree seemed to know this. Pulling itself together it slowly got its roots round the spikes, which I have never been able to remove. Twenty-four years on it has become the beautiful tree I'd hoped for, with its branches reaching towards my bedroom. It is beloved by me and the birds, a tree which perfectly illustrates those who trust in God as we read in Isaiah Chapter 26 v3; and the Hebrew for 'stayed'[1] is 'staked'.

Just as the Ostria grew so did our 'Farm'. In five years our six acres had become home for 20 cattle, mostly Dexters and Red Polls, of all ages and a small flock of sheep, I had long given up teaching, registered the holding in my name, so we could obtain any available subsidies and it had begun paying its way. Poor Michael was still teaching to pay the mortgage, with much added responsibility. On top of being Head of Science for two schools, his week-ends, 'holidays' and evenings were also busy; for as you can imagine farm work, like women's work, is never done. Something had got to give and in Mike's case it meant his resignation! Having been told that he would have a fatal stroke if he did not leave work at once, he came home with a tiny pension (he was only in his 40's) and a lump sum.

But Romans 8:28 was still in 'The Book', because at that precise time all of Station Farm's land came back on the market. An unheard of event – little farms once sold off to big land owners <u>never</u> normally reappear. But this farmer was in money trouble with two mortgages called in; <u>and</u> we needed more land to make a living. I'm afraid I wasn't prepared to go back to teaching – my cows gave me homework I know, but I didn't have to do the marking. A very big plus!

So Mike's precious money and a large bank loan secured for us the heart of Station Farm; we bought the brick and tile barns, the deep well, and 30 more acres. Soon we were to have 40 head of cattle, and 150 sheep, when all lambed, and a full-time life for both us. As head of pasture, Mike restored and used a Grey Ferguson tractor, fertiliser spreader and mower. He was also 'Lord High Everything Else' in his roles as electrician, builder, carpenter and of course gardener. His blood pressure lowered and the strain left his face.

I was 'Cowsbody-in-Chief' and Shepherd, and waitress and lavatory attendant on a vast scale. If my father had known I would spend $^1/_3$ of my winter days mucking out, (did you know a cow/bull does a cowpat every two hours the entire 24 hours? I'm sure you'll find that fact useful sometime), he would have laughed even more, and hoped to put me off!

We hardly left the Farm, except to sail on our beloved estuary, and for four years the Dream was going along nicely for both of us. But God's Plans for the rest of Station Farm were far from realized. There were bad dreams and even nightmares ahead, alongside the joys and love so many animals were to bring.

[1] A.V. (King James Authorised Version)

14

CHAPTER 7

MURPHY'S LAW

The weaned bull calves, who were now in the big 100' x 40' overflow yard, were doing well. One really handsome and strong chap was the picture of health and after they'd all eaten their tea, he'd lead the evening knees up. Charging up and down, chasing the chickens, and play fighting, they put on a good show.

At breakfast, the next morning I was surprised to see him still lying down over by the back of the yard. On reaching his side I could see he was long dead, - his head twisted round. He'd probably collided with the wall at speed and broken his neck. Murphy's Law had been in operation, because he just had to be the best bull on the Farm. Our fallen, broken world throws this up for us all the time. It happens in our own lives often enough and it was soon to do so in Mike's.

Two years after I'd met Cancer head on, Michael was also diagnosed with it and in his case, despite aggressive treatment and an operation which took away his voice, he was not to recover. Murphy's Law seemed to have got the wrong one again in my eyes. Mike had loved and trusted his Shepherd since he was 12, and never been unfaithful. Whereas I for 20 years or so, had taken back control of my life and gone my own way. My Cancer had been the best thing that could have happened, for I turned back to God and asked Him to let me come to Heaven. Death had again brought me to my spiritual senses. How we need to "number our days to gain a heart of wisdom", as David wrote in Psalm 90:12. I had expected to die, for at 50, cancer can spread so quickly. Indeed I felt I deserved to die, not Michael. But of course, he is now with his Lord and safe forever and much better off without me! No more 'just jobs' – you know the sort – 'Could you just do so and so for me?'

A year after Mike's death my beloved Uncle died leaving me a legacy at exactly the same time as the rest of Station Farm's land, almost 70 acres, again came back on the market. The landowner had found it uneconomic to trail his machines back and forth. God had organised and timed all this as I wrote in my earlier 'Further Shepherd's Yarns'. I could not afford all that acreage, but made a joint bid with two men who wanted to set up a Cider Apple Orchard. Our friendship has united the farm and provided a grassland oasis for tame and wild life. It's an unheard of event and very definitely against Murphy's Law, God was in control because "His Plans stand for firm

15

forever!" Psalm 33:11. Mind you, two of my large landowning neighbours had thought their bids would be accepted but "no plan of God's can be thwarted." Job 42:2.

CHAPTER 8
THE ELYSIAN FIELD

Well-grown, healthy pasture looks good enough to eat and I've often felt like getting a knife and fork and tucking in, especially once the newly sown 20-acre field, I had bought with Uncle's money, had grown to perfection. It was ideal sheep grazing and their nibbling would help it to tiller. My flock was on a rather bare meadow and had watched me fencing and checking all was ready for them to start on the feast, and moving day had arrived.

So after calling the ewes and lambs up, I opened their gate and set off, rattling a food sack to alert any dawdlers. Once in the new field I quickly realised I only had about ½ a dozen old faithful ewes at my side. The rest were clustered at their gateway refusing to move. Didn't I realise they'd never been that way before and going through the little woodland was a step too far?

I sighed and set off for my German Shepherd Dog so I could activate Plan B. He was sent round behind the flock so as to urge them to follow me. Deadlock again; and Plan C where I enlisted the help of my two Apple Orchard friends, had the same result.

It was a ridiculous situation so I decided to leave both field gates open overnight, for surely they would mosey in, tempted by the lush pasture.

The next morning saw all the flock still on their old field and in desperation I rang a friend, who had proper sheepdogs, to come and sort us out. I'm ashamed to report that many of my ewes turned on the unsuspecting collies as they protected their infants. I only hoped this wouldn't ruin all the training these dogs had been patiently given.

I now only had Plan F left, I trailed off for my old van which we then used to ferry all the sheep across the divide. Catching and hauling all of them into the vehicle and then unloading each one was very hot and hard work. It took us hours and by the end we were both cross and exhausted. Of course as soon as the flock found themselves plonked in their 'Five Star Restaurant' they ate non-stop, relishing their taste of heaven.

We had forced my sheep that day, they had no choice. But I kept thinking of Our Lord's parable about the Wedding Feast (in Paradise) and his invitation.[1] We have the dignity of free-will and can refuse His R.S.V.P.

There is an inheritance ahead beyond our wildest dreams, and I hope no one reading this throws that away.

[1.] Matthew 22:1-16

CHAPTER 9
ROXY AND SISSY

I got a shock as I peered into the trailer. Surely, Mike (the head Dairyman at the farm from where I get my bull calves) had brought me the biggest cow in the world! She filled the inside, towering above me, and alarm bells began ringing as I considered my ability to handle her. Whatever had I let myself in for? She in turn, was not impressed with what Station Farm had to offer.

First of all where was the grass? After three months of drought, the worst Spring in living memory, my fields were bare and everyone was back on hay and straw. She had always been given the best of everything from maize silage and highly productive grazing, to the most nutritious cattle cake and quality hay. And here I was expecting her to eat sugar beet nuts, oats and straw! It was a disgrace! Didn't I realise who she was? Roxanne Crichel is an aristocratic Holstein who has given her farmer heifer calves worth thousands, not to say 100 tons of milk in 12 years. (That's over 10 gallons a day, by the way!) So how could she let such food pass her lips! She almost certainly didn't know what I could see stamped on her behind. She rather inelegantly bears the plain number 92 on her rump. So I wasn't fooled by her Prima Donna response.

I did meekly set off to buy her one sack of the best coarse food I could find. It's a kind of muesli; it looked and smelt better than mine and she eventually deigned to give it a try. But I guessed, rightly as it turned out, a 92, who got hungry enough, would soon join in at the bull troughs.

On her first day, I led out to a little field and put her with a small herd of Donkeys. But that was my second gaffe. She COULD NOT associate with such hoi polloi – where was her own family? She was lonely, bewildered and a bit cross. She'd always been in the hands of men and here was some woman, trying to call her by name (I was using 'ROXY') and even waving a brush about in an attempt at grooming. A lot of undignified nonsense! But slowly she responded and began accepting me as Boss. Just think of it, a huge, lumbering, gentle giant of nearly a ton yielding to an 8¾ stone weedlet who couldn't even see over her shoulders!

My third faux pas was the last straw. How could I expect her to cope with FLIES – especially the horsey sort? She had always been protected from such pests in the past. So taking the law into her own hooves, she regularly broke back through two electric fences to retreat into the back of her loose box and hide.

Once the grass grew, temperatures lowered, and flies decreased, I put her with a group of bulls and a cow of mine called Xena. She then decided to settle down to the retirement she'd been planning all along. At 15, a remarkable age for a dairy cow who has had to work so hard, she had refused to get in calf again, and I for one didn't blame her and that's why I've found a space for her with me.

Roxy and the Bulls (Impossi/Bull)

Roxy had been given no choice over her move to Station farm, but an animal of a very different kind and size very deliberately decided this was the place she wanted to live in. It was about five years ago that she, along with her mother and brother were 'tipped out' somewhere in my woods. (Cat-tipping is as rife here as fly-tipping is elsewhere). Whether or not the kittens were actually born on the farm, I don't know but somehow they'd been reared through three harsh winter months. Then Mum had fallen foul of a neighbouring Gamekeeper who'd shot her on my land as I was to discover the following Spring. Her two babies may have seen this happen, and somehow in their loneliness and fear they had worked their way down the hedges, ½ mile to the house and barns. Their journey was fraught with dangers, including crossing the lane, and ending in the garden and meeting my Alsatian. He has always lived with cats, but can't resist a chase and gets very excited. As he did the day he dashed up to me and 'told' me "there's a cat over there you know!"

A day later I had trapped a small, very fluffy, dark tabby. It was starving and scared, and showed no sign of trusting me or taming down despite enjoying the bed and breakfast (and of course, lavatory attendance) but it was not going to repay me with its love.

I tried hard for five weeks to get somewhere and had just decided it was already too feral to enjoy a home, when my dog told me there was another cat about. It was so starving (and small) that it went into a baited rabbit trap. It was a mirror image of the first kitten, so I thought... "Ah! A litter mate of the first, I'll put them together and that will help both to settle down." How wrong I was! After a couple of days of much spitting and growling the first demanded OUT.

So now, I turned to the second little mite. At her next feed, she came out of hiding, behind a desk and ate calmly in front of me! The other one had never done that. After she'd scoffed the lot, she then started to play with a toy I was dangling. In a short while, she rolled over and wanted her tummy tickling. This was a miracle! She had been out, alone, for 5 extra weeks (goodness knows what she'd eaten!) and cats quickly become fearful and wild, and need kid-glove handling and much time and patience. Even then, it's often a failure.

How wise of Sissy, as I have named her, to make such a choice. For as far as I can guarantee she has a loving home for life, while sadly her brother's future was 'bleak', with trigger happy farming neighbours all around, should he wander.

Their story is another one for us to consider and takes me back to the previous chapter. And for me Sissy is a delight, she is the most loving cat I've ever known and beautiful with it and her huge fluffy tail is like a banner of joy.

Her choice to enjoy life here fits The Dream perfectly. She sees Station Farm as her sanctuary of peace and safety with large dollops of love thrown in. My 3-year-old wish in a nutshell!

CHAPTER 10

SAPPHIRE

It was 3.00 a.m. on a beautiful moonlit February night, cold and frosty, when I was jerked awake by a very loud and insistent Moo. It was a voice I knew well – I knew all my cows (and ewes) in this way. This is because they are unique with their own D.N.A., just like us. So everything about them is also unique. Nose prints, markings, even character. D.N.A. is Design Not Accident - too complicated not to have a Designer. So all of us have been made in Heaven, in love, and are special.

So here was May, a retired Dexter telling me to, get up quickly and do something. If you are a cowsbody and you hear mooing at night it always means trouble, especially if several individuals are calling! You must take action, and I certainly did, grabbing layers and rushing downstairs. On opening the back door I heard a voice I didn't recognise. It was high pitched, effeminate and inveigling. 'Must be an escapee, who has reached the farm,' I thought, 'definitely not one of mine'. On reaching the lane I could see it was one of mine! It was Sapphire, (yes! I'd got to the S year) May's adolescent and very nubile daughter! She was mincing along, looking down at the buildings where all 40 of the rest of the cattle were housed at night; they were out in the yard watching this moonlit star-performance and the bull was especially impressed. He was cheering her on in that deep sweet – talking rumbling only a bull can do.

I had to DO something; and quick! Because it wasn't going to be long before Jackson would have that 12' x 5' gate off its hinges and bring everyone up to the road and over the little fence. Rushing off to get some bait, I then began waving a parsnip about and calling Sapphire, who mercifully knew her name. At first her mind was too blown to respond, but once I'd virtually pushed a carrot up her nose she turned and took one after another as I led her back to the House field and to her mother, where I firmly shut her up. If you're thinking I was a bit of a spoilsport, you're right. But at 13 (in our years) she was a bit young for such hanky-panky!

I don't remember my picture books on farms telling me about such goings on, but I know my father would have enjoyed the story. I think my mother would have had a fit! But I like the fact that a Cowsbody's life is never dull. The commitment and discipline which are necessary agree with me, but those concepts are not popular to-day. They were in the Apostle

Paul's eyes and he "pressed on towards the goal to win the prize for which God was calling him heaven wards"[1], urging us to do the same. I wonder if there'll be a prize for Cowsbodys.... I know I have a prize waiting for any cow who'd volunteer to do the some housework. But they are too clever for that I fear.

[1] Philippians 3:14

CHAPTER 11
ME AND MY SHADOWS

The Vet had driven up in a hurry. So dropping everything, I went to meet him guessing he was running late. As I walked up the track to the road, I heard the patter of hooves behind me. And there was Mitey Min, a very faithful ewe I had reared as an orphan (featured in A Shepherd's Yarns) dogging my footsteps. She had squeezed out of the sheep's electric fence, braving the shock, because she couldn't bear to be apart from me for long.

By the way the Vet was frenziedly searching for his equipment I knew I had no time to put her back. As I opened the gate to cross the lane, Mitey Min pushed me aside to make sure she could come as well.

"Right", said the young man I'd never met before, "where's the cow?" She was on a field by the house, so we all set off to find her. The Vet glanced quizzically at my ewe, but before I could explain why a sheep should be coming as well, he launched into details of what injection he would use. It was, hopefully, to prevent Emma, a Dexter prone to milk fever at calving developing the condition. Previously she had collapsed on top of me as I was helping her new born. I ended up squashed, but unscathed and she recovered, but each time it happened put her in more danger.

We went through the two gates on our way to the cattle and arrived at Emma's side. Although sheep are very wary amongst cows Mitey Min was still glued to me. The job done, we then all returned the way we'd come and reached the vet's car. I was about to try and say why I was acting out 'Mary had a little lamb' (or rather a big fat ewe) when he was saying "Well, must dash, Good-bye Mrs Sparkes", and he was off. I have never seen him since, so what he thought of this mad woman I can only guess!

Actually I was rather pleased with dear Mitey Min's love and closeness. Often she would get a bit too close and somehow get her legs tangled with mine and trip me up! But better that than going her own way and many times she helped me lead the rest of the flock by sticking by my side. You know, I'm sure Our Shepherd would also rather we tripped Him up, than going astray[1]. This sort of shadowing was never more equalled than by a German Shepherd Dog I rescued from our local R.S.P.C.A. Home. I had just lost my great companion and guard, Steel (see Further Shepherd's Yarns), dying of a heart attack. Since thieves are always checking out isolated farms, I need an adult dog as a deterrent. So I went off to the

Kennels to see a young dog of 10 months who had been taken in. Sadly, so often when an Alsatian reaches this age, it becomes a handful and requires a firm hand, which of course, it should have had from puppyhood. After walking and talking to him, I was quite sure I couldn't trust him with the stock or the liberty on the farm. As I was about to set off, one of the girls stopped me and asked if I'd consider another older, G.S.D. that they had. So that's how I came to meet Shadow. (Yes! That really was her name!) She had been badly ill-treated, abandoned in a shed and starved. Would I give her a chance? 'Now look,' I thought, 'I need a young dog, not an old bitch, whose sight looks very blurry and whose legs are getting stiff!' But a stronger and more persistent whisper was urging me to take her home. At least, she looked the part in a burglar's eyes and she was quiet and very obedient – a definite plus for life on the farm.

She didn't need a second bidding; jumping in the truck and travelling happily back with me. Whether or not she had ever met cattle or donkeys I have no idea, but nothing fazed her, as long as I didn't leave her.

By evening on that first day with me, a friend had arrived for a meal and a night's stay. She and I, Shadow and the cats enjoyed our goodies together around the open fire. But after that the rot set in. Joyce and I retired to bed leaving the animals together downstairs.

Then it started. A piercing howl which gathered momentum and was probably heard the mile away in the village! That's when I remembered what was on the form I had signed to re-home Shadow. There was a section headed 'Problems'; under the heading was a brief comment "Howls when left" and how! She was a professional howler. She had learned all the variations and had been practising them in that shed where she had been. She could go on and on and on all day and all night and had done so. The noise sounded as though Station Farm had taken in a pack of wolves. Sleep was impossible and despite several efforts at re-settling her, I had to take drastic action. Reaching for the sedatives I always keep in case, a dog has a bad accident and needs calming – a big dog can obviously be very dangerous if in pain and needing help, I was able to give Shadow a good night's rest and us as well.

The next night was a repeat performance which Joyce was spared! By the third night my nerves were frayed; she was still in good voice, and I didn't like to give her yet another tablet. So... if you can't beat 'em join 'em was the only solution. I joined her downstairs – she in her cosy bed by the Rayburn me on the dining room floor on a mattress. She slept blissfully happy, but I was cold and uncomfortable and fed up. So after waking for the

26

umpteenth time and listening to her snores I made a decision, I said quite loudly and firmly to our Father God: "I can't go on like this, I need my sleep, because I work so hard. I believe you meant me to care for this dog. So please help. If you don't stop her howling tomorrow night, I shall have to take her back the next day. It won't be fair on her to keep her any longer."

The next night before going to bed, I took her upstairs showed her where I slept, then back down. If you are thinking why I didn't let her sleep upstairs too, you have perhaps never owned a G.S.D. they get up and down a lot, very noisily and snore enough to wake the dead. Must be to do with that big nose. Well as I was waiting in bed for the first howl ("O ye of little faith")[2] I fell asleep. Two hours later I woke and realised there was silence! But then I had to get up to the loo; 'That's sure to start her up,' I thought. But, no! Not a sound. And she never howled at night again. It was a MIRACLE! A dog behaviourist would tell you, it could take weeks, even months for a dog, so traumatised, to settle. And some never do. How I was to kick myself, for not asking Our Lord, to also stop her in the day, because she refused to be left in the truck alone. However, I don't think that would have been in His Plans, because when she came into Farm Talks everyone loved her and she acted like His evangelist. They heard about the miracle and what God had done.

Mitey Min and Shadow, in their closeness to me and their enjoyment of the security I and the Farm gave them were the perfect fulfilment of all I had been longing for since my childhood.

[1]·Psalm 63:7,8. A.V. & N.I.V. [2]·Matthew 14:31.

CHAPTER 12
TAKING STOCK

As time has gone on, Station Farm's started to look like a Rest Home for the Elderly – elderly animals that is – the little old lady is still the warden and on call 24/7, 365 days of the year. But at least, I am no longer spending nights in the lambing sheds or out in the fields with the cattle, acting as mid-wife. I have retired my ewes and suckler herd, allowing everyone to live out their days on the farm. Waitressing and Lavatory Attendance still keep me out of mischief and so does all the farm maintenance, but there are slightly less worries and burdens.

Well there were up to six years ago, until the spectre of Inheritance Tax began to haunt me. The person, who I thought might be my heir, could only have stumped up the cash if he had sold off some land or the house. I knew this was not in God's Plans, since He'd performed so many wonders of God-incidences (as opposed to co-incidences) to put the holding back together. He had not made me His Steward here, just to throw it all away; His purposes were going on beyond my life, even on into Eternity, for all I know.

So as His caretaker I had to take some action. That's why the bull calves began to arrive, to maintain the farm's working status. Hopefully that would be enough to gain some reduction in tax. So I was back to full-time duties with new challenges. These are entire bulls and many do not leave the farm until they are young men with strong libidos. Once they are sold on they need to be in secure units and definitely not fed by hand in their midst, as I have to do. With me they learn their group name of 'Boys', so they will come when called and a few commands, especially 'mind', 'no', and 'wait', given in a forceful voice. They need to be kept at bay, to avoid me ending up at the bottom of a rugby scrum.

Unfortunately, this system was to founder and fall apart, just as I was, towards the end of the second winter into the enterprise. Everyone was still being housed overnight, and on winter rations, well into April. There was a great pressure on me first thing in the mornings, to get hungry mouths filled. No one wanted to be the last fed, so my feet hardly touched the ground. What they did touch that fateful morning was a heavy old piece of equipment, as I was badly jostled. I then tripped up and my left arm hit the ironwork with some force. This threw the bucket of food on to the ground, spilling its contents. Mercifully I was amongst the youngest group of bulls, who though eager for the goodies, held back in fear, as I yelled and struggled to get up.

My wrist seemed at an odd angle but I'd no time to pander to it, for I'd barely started on all the morning chores. Later, ice packs, (actually frozen gooseberries) eased it a little, but with all the teas to see to, there was no time for a big fuss.

I'd also had to try a practice 'run' in my truck to see if driving was possible. But gear changing could only be done with my right arm while at a standstill. The 10 miles I was to travel to preach the next day was rather too far in first gear, so a lift would be needed.

I hoped the wrist would have pulled itself together in time for the next morning's work, but of course it hadn't. And later a doctor and two nurses in the congregation, seeing my plight, ordered me off to A&E. Due to the need to get back for everyone's teatime I was dealt with very promptly.

Once plastered I was much more immobile, so a kind farming friend managed to find time to help with the early work for a couple of weeks. The evenings he couldn't do, but God had gone way ahead to prepare someone who would come. Six months before all this to-do, I'd been taking a service and a lady I knew only as Sylvia had, out of the blue, given me her phone number on a scrap of paper, "just in case I ever needed help". She was volunteering her husband and I hoped he knew! Amazingly, I'd kept the note and not washed it with my clothes. So poor Brian was landed right in it! He proved a double blessing, for often when he arrived he was bearing a delicious offering from his wife's cooking. I love the way our Father God never does things by half. "My cup really ran over"[1] with such kindness.

The wrist healed perfectly and I never looked back, but not long after, my elbow decided to upstage it, by getting dislocated as I fell backwards over a fence. Once the plaster came off this time, physiotherapy was needed to lengthen and straighten the tendons. And Station Farm was more than up to the job. Saffy donkey had suffered a bad back accident and required lifting up frequently, so I and kind friends did this for many weeks. It was the best treatment I could have had! Perhaps hospitals should have a donkey on hand in the Physio Department! Sadly, she did not make a recovery and there is no wheel chair or Zimmer frame available for animals of her size.

Before the winter set in that year I took stock (literally). Although for tax purposes, the greater total of cattle on the farm the better, was the aim; I knew God was saying what Jethro advised Moses in Exodus chapter 18 v18b.

"The work is too heavy for you!" I would have to reduce the number of bulls and so I only reared 30 in the next season. However, God's plans did not include the Inland Revenue, and He was to send rooks (not ravens this time) to 'feed'[2] me with His solution.

[1] Psalm 23:5.   [2] 1 Kings 17.

Bull Crossing Patrol

30

CHAPTER 13
DONKEY DREAMS

Big feet always impress me and I am quite pleased that mine are now triple E fitting after years in wellies. They're nearly as broad as they are long! When I think of Roxy Cow's feet I know they'd certainly make an impression if she stepped on you! Even calves, who usually weigh more than me, have squashed and battered my toes as they've casually trod on them. I'm very glad that I never got too close to the owner of the most enormous horseshoe I found here recently. He or she must have been one of those heavy working horses on the old farm photos I have.

Horses were of course, part of my model farm – the likes of Shires, Suffolks or Percherons of which I still stand in awe. Their huge tamed strength is the perfect illustration of our Lord's "meekness".[1] A word we despise to-day as we see it as 'weakness'. But true humility is allowing God to use us in His Will to our full potential, just like a tamed elephant too.

A farming friend has always kept a Suffolk Horse or two. One such was Isla, who worked for him and who he took to shows and fetes in a specially strengthened and heightened trailer. I once had the privilege of sitting on her back almost doing the splits to do so. Sadly, she died of Laminitis, because our pastures are too rich, and this was a merciful warning to me to stop hankering for a heavy horse.

That part of the Dream had to go, but there was still one piece needed to complete the model farm. I was to go to the other extreme in foot size; from EEEEE fitting down to a C. However, if you've read the beginning of all this you will know that even that size packs a punch. I now have 44 of these dainty feet about and they are quicker, sharper and just as painful as any heavy horse's.

But all is forgiven by me and anyone who comes to meet their owners. Donkeys do something to us it seems, whether we're 9 or 90. When people hear their sad histories, hearts go out to them. All eleven on the farm at present have been rescued, even the youngest foals, who were carried here by their pregnant mothers. The two small filly foals have the 'cute factor' par excellence. Especially tiny Pickle a brown bundle of fluff and living up to her name in colour and nature. She is feisty, naughty, and following in Mum Sophie's footsteps. Pickle has a friend in Treacle, Syrup's baby girl. She is grey and is rather like a fluffy Brillo Pad on legs. She is very sweet

31

and loving and a goody two-shoes, who will hopefully bring some order to Pickle's life. There should have been a third little girl to join them, but dear Stephie, the quietest and wisest of the four mares aborted two months early. The gestation is about 13 months, so she had carried her for so long and all through that terrible journey and handling from Ireland. Baby was hairless and had died in the womb. A stark reminder of the trauma they had all been through on their way to the U.K. slaughterers. Stephie was devastated over her loss and constantly comes to me for comfort – her big sad eyes seem to be saying; "I've lost my baby, you know." Susie the fourth mare is yet to foal, or may have absorbed the embryo – it's hard to say.

Tea Time for Pickle

This little Dream of Donkeys lives on the farm, while the other herd of five are at the house. They are a very assorted group – with two oldies, Deidre, the over 40, and Zorina 38, and young Doris and her two very naughty offspring. Sylphie at two and Sam at one, who is like a Hoodie Yob, who incites his sister to create riots. The two aged aunties (a donkey can live to 50 – "donkeys years old" we say) keep out of the way of the Terrible Two. They have each other and are my oldest equine residents.

Deidre came with her adult daughter Blossom, Zorina with her bosom pal Mille, both of whom have died. They also lost their friends Sam, a gelding, and Saffy who had the bad accident. Donkeys can actually pine to death, when they lose a friend and that includes humans. One old gelding for example whose master died, was taken in by the Donkey Sanctuary and to stop him pining he was given his owners wellies, which he took everywhere he went.

When the donkeys come back near the road many people stop and even ask if they can come in and meet them. So I can talk to complete strangers about these living visual aids. They all bear the Cross in their markings – a dark strip down their backs and down their shoulders. This symbol written in their D.N.A. deliberately by their Maker who then rode one (a larger version than our U.K. ones) to His Cross, tells us plainly what He has done for us and how much he loves us. Dying in our place, and then giving us victory over death;[2] this is His free gift to us,[3] and it's a full circle for my life!

The Farm Dream of Donkeys

Since writing this, Susie (on the left in the photo) has had a little colt named Socks.

[1] Matthew 11:29.   [2] 1 Corinthians 15.   [3] Ephesians 2:8

CHAPTER 14

FULL CIRCLE

Very recently that film, of Alfred Hitchcock, 'The Birds' seemed to be showing right here on Station Farm. Hundreds of rooks began invading the fields which became black with them. Not just for a few days, but for three to four months in the autumn, two years running.

Nothing would frighten them away. I tried scarecrows, two very loud gas guns and hours of me playing the part of Worzel Gummidge. I know I actually look right for the role, but the rooks were unimpressed. Even, when a friend of mine came to be Aunt Sally alongside me and shooed with ear splitting cries the birds were unmoved. They would wait until we were on top of them before taking flight. Most would then sit in ranks on the power lines thumbing their noses at us, while the rest slipped away on to another field behind our backs; it was a hopeless task and caused me great despair as I watched them ruining all the well-grazed areas. Over 20 acres were systematically torn up; for rooks have devastating beaks and they made everywhere look like harrowed land.

Their prize for all this effort was Caviar, but to you and me the fat writhing grubs, white with golden heads look revolting, unless, that is, you like maggots. They were the birds' daily meat course and they couldn't get enough of them. They are a type of Cockchafer larvae, hatched from thousands of eggs laid in the Spring when the beetles leave the Oil Seed Rape, which has suddenly become the crop round here. The grubs need grassland and as mine and the Apple Orchard are the only large areas around here, we are invaded.

However, I am glad to say that this year the rooks have been employing another tactic. They set up a May Barbecue, gathering on the pastures waiting to grab the beetles as they emerged from their pupae. Seagulls too came to join in the party and this has greatly cut down the chafer population.

My farm policy has also changed this year on two major counts. First of all, I have kept the grass longer, and so denser, as it has not been over-grazed. This means that the rooks cannot turn it over in the same way as before. This has been possible as stock numbers are much reduced. Those birds have been God's instruments, forcing me to review the farm's future. From being a nightmare, as I watched them ruining the fields, they have brought about the completion of the Dream.

Since the year that the A&E department got fed up with seeing me (I even had to attend a third time after splitting my head open!) a door has miraculously opened for the land itself to take it easier. Yes! "You are the God who performs miracles."[1] He led me to approach a Land Trust who in turn introduced me to a Charitable Trust who in their kindness will take over Station Farm on my death. It will become a nature reserve, with grazing for donkeys and cattle. The precious wild life, which comes to the oasis of safety from the very aggressive agri-business around, will be encouraged. The Barn Owls and Bats will still have their home in the barns, and the land will have peace. And I am smiling again as I think of that day I first voiced my Dream. Why has our Father God so blessed and even bothered with such a piffling little piece of His world? Well, these words of His gave me the answer: "It is a land that the Lord your God cares for... His eyes continually on it from the beginning of the year to the end"[2] Wow! And He has certainly been using it to reach and rescue those who don't know of His saving love. Countless people come to visit the farm; not to see me, but the animals! Especially the donkeys of course! There have been club visits, family visits, and individuals. A WI, for example, turned up one evening and had a never-to-be-forgotten experience of helping me move a group of bulls across the lane. (See photo page 30.) They came after I'd had the privilege of giving them a Farm Talk and so could hear more about what God has done for the Farm and them. Visitors are also fair game for my puns which despite your groans I'm going to share with you.

The first is IRRESISTI/BULL - that's Sapphire of Chapter 10 of course! Then there's INDESTRUCTI/BULL – that's Brian who needs a special mention. He stayed on the farm much longer than most of the Holsteins, because at first he was poorly and weak. When I brought him back to the buildings preparatory to sending him off to his new home, his eyes lit on the big wooden feeder he knew well... Since it was empty, he set upon it, and after a quarter of an hour of a very determined onslaught it was matchsticks! The terrifying cracks as he demolished it were accompanied by much bellowing. A fork lift had been needed to put the huge manger and hay rack in place, but it was definitely NOT indestructible!

The last of these puns (you'll be glad to hear) is IMPOSSI/BULL. I see this regularly when I go to Roxy and the bulls. She's irresistible but they need to be at least 2 feet taller!

If you've been moo/tivated (sorry!) to see that your Dream is not impossible anymore than mine, hang on to it and watch for what God is going to do.

1. Psalm 77:14.   2. Deuteronomy 11:12

36